Do Unto Others ... Then Run

First published in 2001 by Prion Books Ltd
Imperial Works, Perren Street
London NW5 3ED
www.prionbooks.com

ISBN 1-85375-434-X

Cover design by Jon Gray
Printed and bound in Great Britain by
Latimer Trend & Company Ltd., Plymouth

Do Unto Others ... Then Run

a little book of twisted proverbs and sayings

compiled by

Gerd de Ley & David Potter

Proverbs usually read
just as well backwards,
or jumbled up

FRANK SULLIVAN

The pen is mightier
than the sword,
and considerably easier
to write with

Marty Feldman

Never serve rabbit stew
before you catch the rabbit

James Thurber

A bachelor never quite gets
the idea that he is a thing
of beauty and a boy forever

HELEN ROWLAND

Beauty is only skin deep,
but ugly goes clean to the bone

DOROTHY PARKER

Beauty is only sin deep

SAKI (H H MUNRO)

Beauty is in the eye
of the newt and
a hair of the dog

John Lennon

In the beginning there was
no plagiarism

KARL KRAUS

The early bird gets the worm
but look what happens
to the early worm

ALFRED E NEUMAN

The early bird gets the worm,
but the second mouse
gets the cheese

JON HAMMOND

A bird in the hand
can be messy

PETER DARBO

A bird in the hand is dead

RHONDA BOOZER

A bird in the bed
is worth two in the bushes

LAMBERT JEFFRIES

A hair in the head
is worth two in the brush

MILTON BERLE

Don't bite the hand
that lays the golden egg

SAM GOLDWYN

Never judge a book by
its cover price

FRAN LEBOWITZ

Brevity is the soul
of lingerie

Dorothy Parker

You ought to take the bull
between the teeth

SAM GOLDWYN

There's no business
like show business
but there are several
businesses like accounting

DAVID LETTERMAN

It is easier for a camel to pass
through the eye of a needle
if it is lightly greased

JOHN NESVIG

When the cat's away,
chances are he's been run over

Michael Saunders

Children under twelve
must be accompanied
by money

JAMES DENT

Women should be
obscene and not heard

JOHN LENNON

I came, I saw, I concurred

IRVINE H PAGE

Comedy is 90 per cent
perspiration and
10 per cent agents' fees

WAYNE COTTER

Comment is free,
but facts are on expenses

Tom Stoppard

Don't count your chickens
before they cross the road

CHARLES A BELOV

In the country of the blind,
the one-eyed man
has difficulty finding
a good optician

Maxim Décharné

Properly organized,
even crime pays

JIM FISK & ROBERT BARRON

Crime does not pay
as well as politics

ALFRED E NEUMAN

I think crime pays.
The hours are good,
you travel a lot

WOODY ALLEN

Make crime pay,
become a lawyer

WILL ROGERS

Dead owls don't give a hoot

MILTON BERLE

The shortest distance
between two points is
usually under construction

Ryan Showers

Do unto yourself as your
neighbours do unto themselves
and look pleasant

George Ade

Do unto others,
... then run

BENNY HILL

You can't teach an
old dogma new tricks

DOROTHY PARKER

Work is the curse of
the drinking classes

OSCAR WILDE

Early to bed, and early to rise,
and you'll meet very few
of our best people

GEORGE ADE

Early to rise, and early to bed,
makes a male healthy and
wealthy and dead

JAMES THURBER

Eat, drink, and be merry,
for tomorrow ye diet

William Gilmour

Don't put all your eggs
into one bastard

DOROTHY PARKER

To err is human,
but it feels divine.

MAE WEST

To err is human,
to forgive supine

S J PERELMAN

When choosing between two evils
I always like to take the one
I've never tried before

MAE WEST

Forgive your enemies,
but remember their names

JOHN F KENNEDY

Familiarity
breeds
attempt

Jane Ace

First things first, but not necessarily in that order

John Flanagan
& Andrew McCulloch

A friend in need
is a pest, get rid of him

Tommy Cooper

The future
isn't as far away
as it used to be

DALE MARSHALL

Gentlemen
prefer bonds

ANDREW MELLON

If God wanted us to fly,
he would have given us
tickets

MEL BROOKS

If God had intended us
to be nudists,
we would have been born
with no clothes on

LEONARD LYONS

If the good God didn't want us
to eat meat, he wouldn't
have invented mustard

JIMMY PERRY

Oh Lord, forgive them anyway,
although they know damned well
what they are doing

JULIEN DE VALCKENAERE

Many hands want light work

PHILIP J FRANKENFELD

He who hesitates
is last

MAE WEST

History repeats itself.
Historians repeat each other

PHILIP GUEDALLA

Home is where you hang
your head

GROUCHO MARX

Never let a gift horse in the house

LEO ROSTEN

Imitation is the sincerest form
of television

FRED ALLEN

A journey of a thousand miles
begins with a delay
of about three hours

MILTON BERLE

Know thyself.
If you need help,
call the CIA

Mort Sahl

Know yourself
and keep quiet about it

H F H Henrichs

He who laughs last
didn't get it

HELEN GIANGREGORIO

He who laughs, lasts

MARY PETTIBONE POOLE

A lie has short legs
but runs faster than the truth

ANTONI MARIANOWICZ

Life begins at forty
but so does arthritis and
the habit of telling the same story
three times to the same person

SAM LEVENSON

It is better to have loved and lost
than to have paid for it
and not liked it

HIRAM KASTEN

It is better to have loafed and lost
than never to have loafed at all

JAMES THURBER

Better to have loved a short man
than never to have loved a tall

DAVID CHAMBLESS

The fastest way to a man's heart
is through his chest

ROSEANNE BARR

So little time,
so little to do

Oscar Levant

Pity the meek,
for they shall inherit the earth

DON MARQUIS

The meek shall inherit the earth
but not the mineral rights

J PAUL GETTY

The lack of money
is the root of all evil

George Bernard Shaw

Love thy neighbour as thyself,
but choose your neighbourhood

LOUISE BEAL

There is nothing new
under the sun,
but there are lots of old things
we don't know

AMBROSE BIERCE

No news is good news;
no journalists is even better

Nicolas Bentley

A man's only as old as
the woman he feels

GROUCHO MARX

Always a bridesmaid
never a couplet

JOHN LENNON

TB or not TB
that is the congestion

WOODY ALLEN

A penny saved is
a penny

DONALD R WOODS

Never put off until tomorrow
what can be avoided altogether

ANN LANDERS

A watched pot
is usually owned by
someone without cable

PHILIP J FRANKENFELD

Ready, fire, aim

Spike Milligan

All roads lead to rum

W C Fields

Rome wasn't burned in a day

LEO ROSTEN

Rulers were made to be broken

Michael Isenberg

As you sew,
so shall you rip

PHILIP J FRANKENFELD

If the shoe fits
buy the other one too

Johnny Carson

Show me a man with
both feet on the ground,
and I'll show you a man
who can't put his pants on

JOE E LEWIS

If at first you don't succeed,
do it the way your wife
told you to

YVONNE KNEPPER

If at first you don't succeed,
pretend you weren't trying

Mitch Murray

If at first you don't succeed,
try, try again. Then quit.
No use being a damn fool about it

W C FIELDS

Behind every successful man
is a woman.
Behind her is his wife

GROUCHO MARX

Nothing recedes like success

WALTER WINCHELL

Nothing succeeds like address

Fran Lebowitz

Capitalism is
survival of the fattest

Paul Smith

Lead us not into temptation.
Just tell us where it is

SAM LEVENSON

Lead me not into temptation;
I can find the way myself

RITA MAE BROWN

I think, therefore I'm single

LIZ WINSTON

I'm pink, therefore I'm Spam

STEPHEN GRISCOM

Time wounds all heels

JANE ACE

Time flies like an arrow.
Fruit flies like a banana

GROUCHO MARX

Two is company.
Three is fifty bucks

JOAN RIVERS

Virtue has its own reward,
but no box office

MAE WEST

Women: can't live with them,
can't bury them in the back yard
without the neighbours seeing

SEAN WILLIAMSON

The world's a stage
and most of us are
desperately unrehearsed

SEAN O'CASEY

Two rights don't make a wrong,
but three will get you
back on the freeway

JAMES WESLEY JACKSON

A closed mouth
gathers no foot

BOB COOKE

Discretion is
the better part of Valerie,
but all of her is nice

ROGER MCGOUGH

Cleanliness is next to impossible

AUDREY AUSTIN

A fool and his money
are soon married

CAROLYN WELLS

Necessity is
the smotherer of invention

LAMBERT JEFFRIES

Birth was the death of him

SAMUEL BECKETT

If one hides one's talent under
a bushel, one must be careful
to point out the exact bushel
under which it is hidden

SAKI (H H MUNRO)

See a pin and pick it up and all day long you'll have a pin

Audrey Austin

Blood is thicker than water –
and considerably more difficult
to get out of the carpet

WOODY ALLEN

Clothes make the man.
Naked people have little or
no influence on society

Mark Twain

People who live in glass houses
have to answer the doorbell

BRUCE PATTERSON

Give a man a free hand
and he'll run it all over you

Mae West

Go! And never darken
my towels again

GROUCHO MARX

PRION HUMOUR

IF YOU ARE INTERESTED IN RECEIVING DETAILS ABOUT PRION'S humour titles ranging from postcard books to quotation books to the Prion Humour Classics series, please write to the free-post address below, with the details of your name and address. You will receive a regular newsletter containing forthcoming title information, reviews, extracts and special offers. Please note that the freepost address only applies to correspondents within the United Kingdom, when no stamp is required. Overseas readers should please use our full address and the correct postage.

FOR UK CORRESPONDENTS:
PRION HUMOUR
FREEPOST LON12574
LONDON NW5 1YR

OR EMAIL YOUR DETAILS TO: humour@prion.co.uk